Back On The

The Whole Story Of Humpty Dumpty

Written and Illustrated
by Michael Snee

"With God, all things are possible."

— Matthew 19:26 (KJV)

In 1865, the state of Ohio adopted the motto: *An Empire within an Empire.*

Two years later it was dismissed because it sounded too "royal," leaving Ohio with no state motto for 90 years.

In 1956, a nine-year-old boy from Cincinnati suggested a new motto. It was taken from the Bible's book of Matthew 19:26

and for the next three years the boy kept trying to persuade state law makers to accept it.

Finally, in 1959, the Ohio General Assembly adopted his suggestion:

With God, All Things Are Possible – making it Ohio's official state motto.

With thanks to GOD, this book is dedicated with love to every child who will **BELIEVE.**

See more at: **HumptySurvived.com**

© 2005 Michael Snee   First Edition   All Rights Reserved
Library of Congress Control Number: 2006908697
ISBN: 13: 978-0-9789896-0-6

Printed in the United States by Bookmasters Inc
30 Amberwood Parkway, Ashland OH 44805
April 2012, Job number M9526

Humpty Dumpty sat on a wall.
Humpty Dumpty had a great fall.
All of us children through all of our lives
Were taught that poor Humpty had never survived.

– Until now.

UMPTY DUMPTY sat on a wall.

UMPTY DUMPTY had a great fall.

LL the king's horses and all the king's men

Couldn't put Humpty together again.

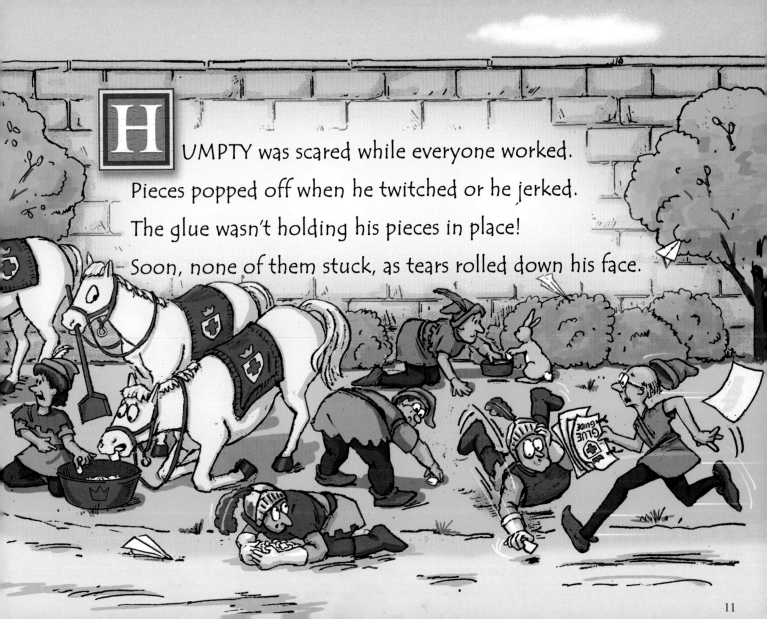

HUMPTY was scared while everyone worked.

Pieces popped off when he twitched or he jerked.

The glue wasn't holding his pieces in place!

Soon, none of them stuck, as tears rolled down his face.

LL the king's horses and all the king's men

Told Humpty Dumpty, "You'll never again

Go for a walk or ever play ball.

You are too broken to stand up at all."

HEY brought some warm soup, feeding him slow.

Soon it was evening and most had to go.

Humpty wanted to move, but fearing the worst,

Thought to himself, *I might crumble or burst!*

HUMPTY just laid there, year after year.

Crying and worried, he prayed out of fear.

Then one sunny day someone special came by.

His name was Jesus and he stopped to say, "Hi."

"ELLO, Humpty Dumpty! I know about you.

You cry all the time and your tears melt the glue."

"It's because of what happened," Humpty replied.

"I fell off this wall – and I almost died!"

"I climbed many times and sat up on that wall.

Why did I NOW have such a great fall?

It's not my fault I'm broken and sad

With all of these cracks ,,, and feeling so bad."

"**A**LL the king's horses and all the king's men

Kept gluing my pieces again and again.

But they should have tried harder – with all kinds of stuff."

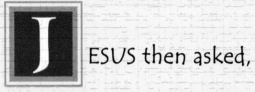ESUS then asked,

"Well, have YOU done enough?"

" UMPTY, you learned how to get on this wall.

Now you can learn to survive a great fall.

Believe that GOD sent me to teach something true.

BELIEVE I can save you – and save others, too."

"OD is your friend who can show you new ways

To find happy things in your life every day!

GOD always helps me. He will always help you.

Learn of his love and BELIEVE it is true!"

T HEN Jesus said, "I'll teach you to mend.

Believe you are worthy to have GOD as your friend!

Believe in your heart as never before.

GOD loves the birds, but loves YOU even more."

"**B**ELIEVE in yourself! Believe GOD heals your scars!

Believe GOD's by your side! You'll climb to the stars!

Believe that GOD loves you! You won't feel so sad.

BELIEVE it! Then good things can come from the bad!"

"**Y**OU have a choice to feel better, not bitter.

Choose to BELIEVE! Don't be a quitter.

Believe in GOD's love and soon you will see

His power unlocked! Your FAITH is the key!"

UMPTY chose FAITH. He started to pray.

"Dear GOD I believe you will help me some way.

You are my friend, though I'm not always good.

Please heal my cracks. Jesus told me you could."

"GOD put his Spirit in you," Jesus said.

"Now learn to listen, so you won't be misled.

The Spirit will teach and remind you of things

That deal with GOD's love, and the hope that it brings."

THE Spirit said softly, "GOD doesn't lie.

Get it together. Don't just get by.

Others can't fix all your pieces with glue.

Some pieces won't stick – unless held there by you."

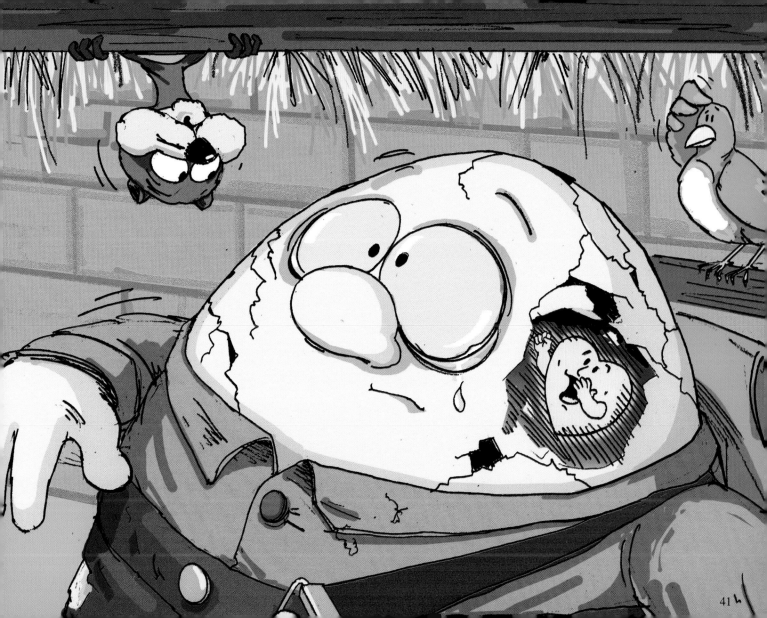

UMPTY listened. He hoped. He held on from inside.

The old glue became sticky – then held his outside!

He giggled. He laughed, then shouted, "Good News!

Now I can wiggle my toes in my shoe!"

HUMPTY struggled to stand, believing he would.

Thanking GOD for his love ... Humpty finally stood!

Then all the king's horses and all the king's men

Cheered to see Humpty now standing again!

UMPTY learned more of GOD's love deep and wide.

He learned more about Jesus and GOD's Spirit, inside.

He learned FAITH lifts you up and erases a frown

And when you BELIEVE – fear can't hold you down.

OW Humpty helps others with clothing and food.

Doing good deeds to brighten their mood.

The more he helps others, just as he should,

It brings them a smile and makes him feel good.

UMPTY has learned and wants you to know,

GOD's always there and willing to show

How to get it together and not lay in pieces.

Believe in yourself ... by trusting in Jesus!

UMPTY DUMPTY is back on the wall

Like many of us who have had a great fall.

People can help us. That's something we need.

But miracles happen ...

      when we learn to BELIEVE!

Proverbs 3:5,6
Trust in the Lord with all your heart and lean NOT on YOUR OWN understanding; in all your ways acknowledge Him...and He will make your paths straight. *(NIV - New International Version)*

Mark 5:36
Ignoring what they said, Jesus told the synagogue ruler, "Don't be afraid; just BELIEVE." *(NIV - New International Version)*

John 12:44
Then Jesus cried out, "When a man BELIEVES in me, he does not BELIEVE in me only, but in the one who sent me.
(NIV - New International Version)

John 3:16
"For God so loved the world, that he gave his only begotten Son, that whosoever BELIEVETH in him should not perish, but have everlasting life." *(KJV - King James Version)*

John 20:29
Then Jesus told him (Thomas), "You BELIEVE because you have seen me. But blessed are those who haven't seen me and BELIEVE anyway." *(TLB - The Living Bible)*

Mark 11:24
"Therefore I tell you, whatever you ask for in prayer, BELIEVE that you have received it, and it will be yours."
(NIV - New International Version)

Matthew 9:28
When Jesus had gone indoors, the blind men came to him, and Jesus asked them, "Do you BELIEVE that I am able to do this?" "Yes, Lord," they replied. Then he touched their eyes and said, "According to your FAITH will it be done to you"; and their sight was restored. *(NIV - New International Version)*

Hebrews 11:1
Now, FAITH is being sure of what we hope for ... and CERTAIN of what we do not see. *(NIV - New International Version)*

What is Faith? It is the confident assurance that something we want is going to happen. It is the certainty that what we hope for is waiting for us, even though we cannot see it up ahead. *(TLB - The Living Bible)*

2 Timothy 1:7
For God has not given us a spirit of fear; but of power, and of love, and of a sound mind. *(KJV - King James Version)*

John 5:3-6
(at the pool of Bethesda) Here a great number of disabled people used to lie – the blind, the lame, the paralyzed. One who was there had been an invalid for thirty-eight years. When Jesus saw him lying there and learned that he had been in this condition for a long time, he asked him, "Do you want to get well?" *(NIV - New International Version)*

Matthew 14:29-31
"Come," he said. Then Peter got down out of the boat, walked on the water and came toward Jesus. But when Peter saw the wind, he was afraid and, beginning to sink, cried out, "Lord, save me!" Immediately Jesus reached out his hand and caught Peter. "You of little faith," Jesus said, "Why did you doubt?" *(NIV - New International Version)*

Matthew 13:57,58
And they became angry at him. Then Jesus told them, "A prophet is honored everywhere except in his own country, and among his own people!" And so he did only a few great miracles there, because of their UNBELIEF.
(TLB - The Living Bible)

Matthew 6:26
"Look at the birds! They don't worry about what to eat—they don't need to sow or reap or store up food—for your heavenly Father feeds them. And you are far more valuable to him than they are." *(TLB - The Living Bible)*

James 2:14-17
What good is it, my brothers, if a man claims to have faith but has no deeds? Can such faith save him? Suppose a brother or sister is without clothes and daily food. If one of you says to him, "Go, I wish you well; keep warm and well fed," but does nothing about his physical needs, what good is it? In the same way, faith by itself, if it is not accompanied by action, is dead.
(NIV - New International Version)

Romans 5:1-2
Therefore, since we have been justified through faith, we have peace with God through our Lord Jesus Christ, through whom we have gained access by faith into this grace in which we now stand. And we rejoice in the hope of the glory of God.
(NIV - New International Version)

John 14:26,27
But the Counselor, the Holy Spirit, whom the Father will send in my name, will teach you all things and remind you of everything I have said to you. *(NIV - New International Version)*

Mark 12:29-31
"The most important commandment is this: 'Love the Lord your God with all your heart and with all your soul and with all your mind and with all your strength.' The second is this: 'Love your neighbor as yourself.' There is no commandment greater than these." *(NIV - New International Version)*

Matthew 19:26
Jesus looked at them and said, "With man this is impossible, but with God all things are possible."
(NIV - New International Version)

Philippians 4:13
I can do all things through Christ who strengthens me.
(NKJV - New King James Version)

Just like Humpty, we all sit on walls and sometimes we fall, too.
But falling is *NOT* failing. Ups and downs are just a part of everyone's life.
Read what happens to Billy and Susie as they grow up and experience some ups and downs.
That's why it's important to "BELIEVE."

- **Billy is learning to walk.**
  Oopsey, daisy!

- **Billy found a quarter on the sidewalk this morning.**
  This afternoon, he failed his math test.

- **Billy thinks he'll make the team.**
  He's cut because he doesn't measure up.

- **Billy wants to be a father.**
  His tests reveal complications.

- **Billy changes companies to get a pay increase.**
  The new company lowers costs and Billy loses his job.

- **Billy takes his nephews bowling.**
  He clutches his chest at the foul line.

- **Susie is riding her bike.**
  She falls and scrapes her knee.

- **Susie received an A in English.**
  She's picked last when they choose sides for volleyball.

- **Susie hopes that cute boy will ask her to the prom.**
  He asks someone else instead.

- **Susie has a wonderful wedding.**
  After two children, she gets divorced.

- **Susie's daughter gives birth to a healthy boy.**
  Susie's mother dies the following day.

- **Susie enjoys living by herself.**
  Her children want to put her in a home.

Believe!
Trust God every step of the way.

Follow Michael's blog at HumptySurvived.com

In 1978, Michael Snee began reading nursery rhymes to his two young daughters. After repeated readings of Humpty Dumpty, Michael became concerned with its tragic ending and hopeless message. He wondered what effect this well-known and seemingly innocent story might have on his children and their outlook on life. Was Humpty teaching that you shouldn't climb? Or was it teaching failure and giving up?

Because his children were too young to read, Michael started to invent positive endings to Humpty before turning the page. Added verses grew in meaning, eventually giving the idea for *Back On The Wall*.

Michael is a graphic designer with his own advertising business and occasionally teaches art at area universities.

MATTHEW 19:26

56